MATH FOR
MINECRAFTERS

Adventures in Addition & Subtraction

Illustrated by Amanda Brack

Sky Pony Press
New York

Sky Pony Press books may be purchased in bulk at special discounts for sales promotion, corporate gifts, fund-raising, or educational purposes. Special editions can also be created to specifications. For details, contact the Special Sales Department, Sky Pony Press, 307 West 36th Street, 11th Floor, New York, NY 10018 or info@skyhorsepublishing.com.

Sky Pony® is a registered trademark of Skyhorse Publishing, Inc.®, a Delaware corporation.

Minecraft® is a registered trademark of Notch Development AB.
The Minecraft game is copyright © Mojang AB.

Visit our website at www.skyponypress.com.

Authors, books, and more at SkyPonyPressBlog.com.

10 9 8 7 6 5 4 3 2 1

Cover design by Brian Peterson

Cover illustration by Amanda Brack

Book design by Kevin Baier

Print ISBN: 978-1-5107-1819-7

Printed in China

A NOTE TO PARENTS

When you want to reinforce classroom skills at home, it's crucial to have kid-friendly learning materials. This *Math for Minecrafters* workbook transforms math practice into an irresistible adventure complete with diamond swords, zombies, skeletons, and creepers. That means less arguing over homework and more fun overall.

Math for Minecrafters is also fully aligned with National Common Core Standards for 1st and 2nd grade math. What does that mean, exactly? All of the problems in this book correspond to what your child is expected to learn in school. This eliminates confusion and builds confidence for greater homework-time success!

As an added benefit to parents, the pages of this workbook are color coded to help you target specific skill areas as needed. Each color represents one of the four categories of Common Core math instruction. Use the chart below to guide you in understanding the different skills being taught at your child's school and to pinpoint areas where they may need extra practice.

▚	**BLUE**	Operations and Algebraic Thinking
▚	**PINK**	**Numbers and Operations in Base 10**
▚	**GREEN**	Measurement and Data
▚	**ORANGE**	Geometry

As the workbook progresses, the math problems become more advanced. Encourage your child to progress at his or her own pace. Learning is best when students are challenged, but not frustrated. What's most important is that your Minecrafter is engaged in his or her own learning.

Whether it's the joy of seeing their favorite game characters on every page or the thrill of solving challenging problems just like Steve and Alex, there is something in this workbook to entice even the most reluctant math student.

Happy adventuring!

ADDITION BY GROUPING

Circle Groups of 10. Then count and write the numbers.

Example:

1.

Answer: 26

2.

Answer: _____

3.

Answer: _____

4.

Answer: _____

5.

Answer: _____

MYSTERY MESSAGE
WITH ADDITION
AND SUBTRACTION

Add or subtract. Then use the letters to fill in the blanks below and reveal the answer to Steve's joke.

1. 4 + 8 = **12** S   **6.** 8 - 2 = ____ R

2. 6 - 3 = ____ N   **7.** 9 + 6 = ____ B

3. 3 + 8 = ____ T   **8.** 10 - 3 = ____ L

4. 7 - 5 = ____ M   **9.** 5 + 9 = ____ E

5. 8 + 5 = ____ A

Q: Why do Minecraft horses eat golden apples and carrots with their mouths open?

A: Because they have bad...

COPY THE LETTERS FROM THE ANSWERS ABOVE TO SOLVE THE MYSTERY.

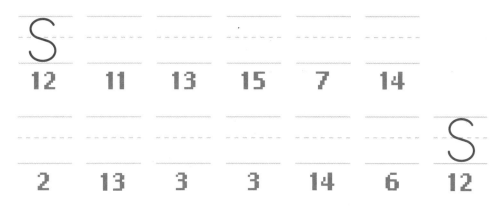

S __ __ __ __ __
12 11 13 15 7 14

__ __ __ __ __ __ S
2 13 3 3 14 6 12

ZOMBIE'S GUIDE TO PLACE VALUE

Use the number on each zombie to fill in the place-value chart. Then, write the number in tally marks.

Example: **1.**

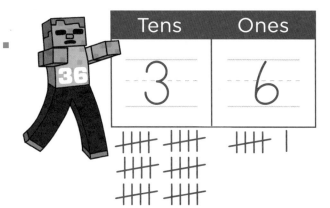

Tens	Ones
3	6

|||| |||| |||| |

2.

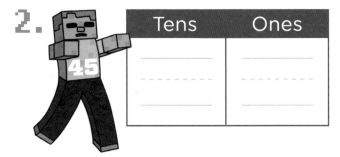

Tens	Ones

3.

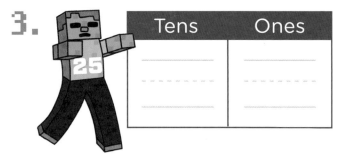

Tens	Ones

4.

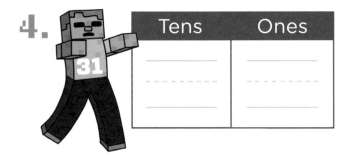

Tens	Ones

5.

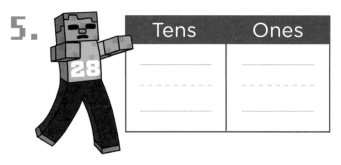

Tens	Ones

6.

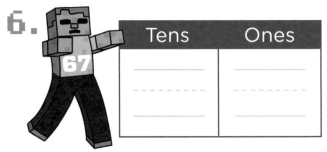

Tens	Ones

7.

Tens	Ones

SKIP COUNT CHALLENGE

Count by 2s and fill in the empty spaces to keep Alex at a safe distance from the cave spider.

2 — 4 — 6 _____

26

TELLING TIME

Look at the clocks below and write the time in the space provided:

Example:

1.

Answer: 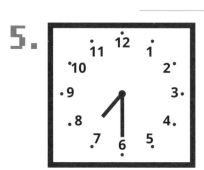 2:00

2.

Answer: _____

3.

Answer: _____

4.

Answer: _____

5.

Answer: _____

6.

Answer: _____

COUNTING MONEY

The villagers are letting you trade coins for emeralds.
Add up your coins to see how much money you have.

25¢   10¢   5¢   1¢

1. 25¢ + 10¢ + 10¢ + 5¢ = **50**¢

2. 10¢ + 5¢ + 5¢ + 1¢ + 1¢ + 1¢ = _____

3. 25¢ + 10¢ + 1¢ = _____

4. 25¢ + 25¢ + 5¢ + 5¢ = _____

5. 10¢ + 10¢ + 10¢ + 5¢ + 1¢ + 1¢ = _____

6. 25¢ + 5¢ + 5¢ + 5¢ + 1¢ = _____

7. 5¢ + 1¢ + 1¢ + 1¢ + 1¢ = _____

HARDCORE MODE: *Try this hardcore math challenge!*

8. One villager charges 25¢ for each emerald. How many (5¢) nickels do you need in order to buy the emerald?

Answer: _____

9

ADVENTURES IN GEOMETRY

Let's learn about fractions! Count the number of squares in the crafting grid below.

Example: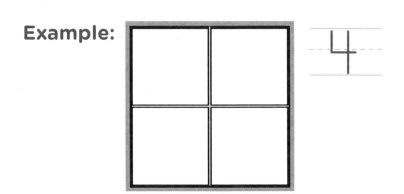

1. Color one of the four squares brown

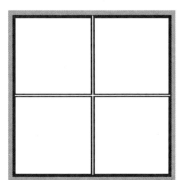

This is called one fourth, or ¼.

2. This crafting grid is divided into two equal parts. Color one of the two parts brown.

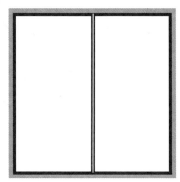

This is called one half, or ½.

3. Count the rectangles in the experience bar below.
Write the number here: _____

4. This experience bar is divided into 3 equal parts.
Color one part green.

This is called one third, or ⅓.

5. This experience bar is divided into 3 equal parts.
Color two parts green.

This is called two thirds, or ⅔.

HARDCORE MODE: *Try this hardcore math challenge!*
A health bar can show up to 10 hearts. Color in 5 hearts below.

Circle the fraction that describes how many are colored in:

A. 1/2   **B.** 1/4   **C.** 1/3

WORD PROBLEMS

Read the problem carefully. Use the picture to help you solve the problem. Fill in your answer.

Example:

You get 10 minutes of daylight in Minecraft. You lose 8 minutes building a shelter and finding food. How many minutes are left?

10 – 8 = 2

Answer: 2 minutes

1. You need 4 wooden planks to make a crafting table, but you only have 3. How many more planks do you need?

Answer: _____

2. There are 9 empty spaces in your inventory bar. You fill 4 spaces with tools. How many empty spaces do you have?

Answer: _____

3. 7 green experience orbs appear. You collect 3 of them. How many orbs are left to collect?

Answer: _____

4. You have 6 sheep on your farm. You add 2 pigs to the farm. How many animals do you have?

Answer: _____

5. You have 7 blocks of sandstone. You get 4 more blocks. How many blocks of sandstone do you have?

Answer: _____

6. 8 creepers are chasing you. 2 of them blow up! How many creepers are still chasing you?

Answer: _____

7. Alex has 7 potions in her inventory. She crafts 2 more potions. How many potions does she have?

Answer: _____

8. Yesterday you attacked 5 zombie pigmen. Today you attacked 8. How many more pigmen did you attack today than yesterday?

Answer: _____

GHAST'S GUIDE TO PLACE VALUE

Read the number on each ghast to fill in the place-value chart. Then, write the number in tally marks.

Example: 1.  **26**

Tens	Ones
2	6

卌 卌   卌 |
卌 卌

2. **43**

Tens	Ones

3.  **35**

Tens	Ones

4. **29**

Tens	Ones

5.  **47**

Tens	Ones

6. **89**

Tens	Ones

7.  **63**

Tens	Ones

SKIP COUNT CHALLENGE

Steve is tired after a long day of mining. Count by 5s and fill in the spaces to help him get home on his new railway system.

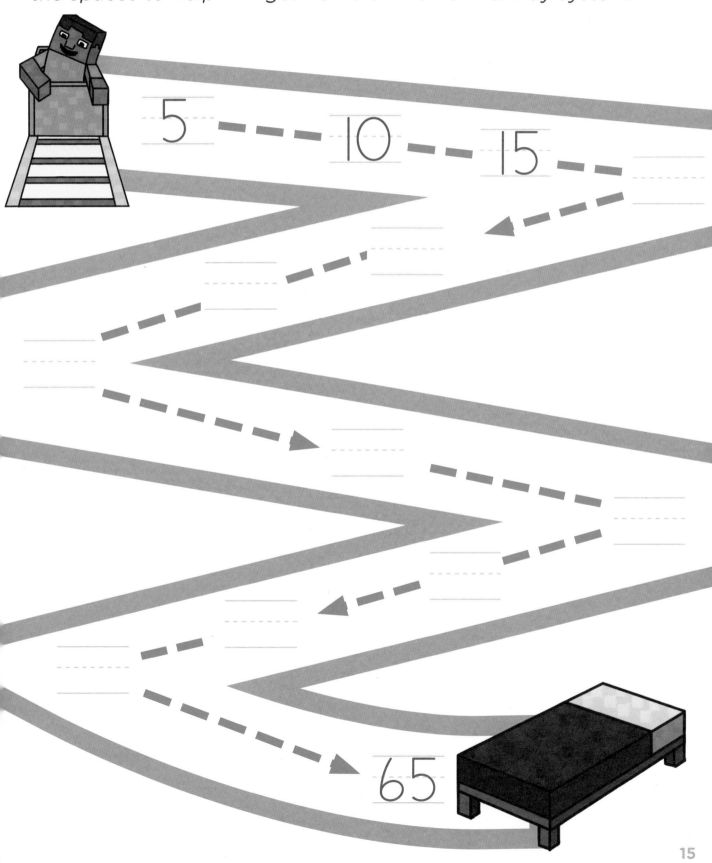

5   10   15

65

ALL IN A DAY'S WORK

A minecrafter's first day is very busy!
Match the time for each task on the left with a clock on the right.

1.  **6:00**
Smash a tree
to get wood.

2. **7:30**
Make a pickaxe.

3.  **9:00**
Get some wool.

4.  **10:00**
Build a bed.

5. **2:30**
Build a shelter.

6. **8:00**
Hear a creeper
hiss nearby.

7. **8:30**
Build a door
fast. Phew!

A.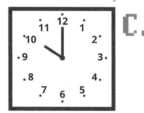

B.

C.

D.

E.

F.

G.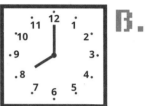

TIME FOR MATCHING

Draw a big hand and a little hand on the clock to show the time.

Example:

3:00

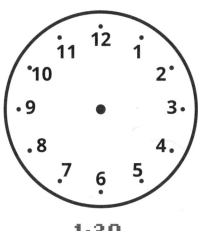

1:30

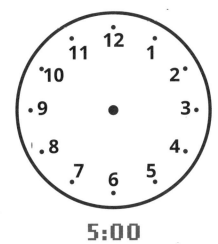

5:00

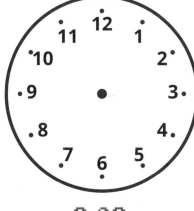

8:30

10:00

4:30

LEARNING ABOUT SHAPES

Draw along the dotted line to complete each shape. Connect the name of the shape to the correct drawing.

1. rectangle

2. square

3. trapezoid

4. triangle

A.

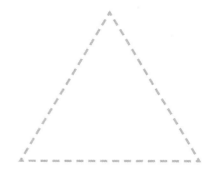

B.

C.

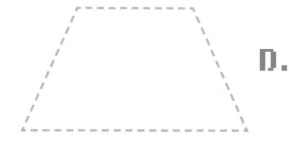

D.

FIND THE SHAPES

Look at the items below and and use the word box to write the name:

square	circle	rectangle

5.

_____

6.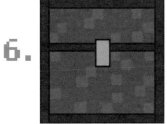

_____

7.

_____

8. HARDCORE MODE: _Try this hardcore math challenge!_

Find 6 rectangles in this bottle of potion.

ADDITION BY GROUPING

Circle groups of 10 weapons and tools. Then count and write the total number.

Example:

1.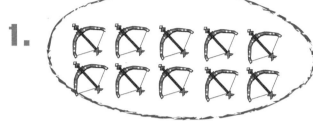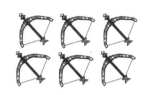

Answer: 16

2.

Answer: _____

3.

Answer: _____

4.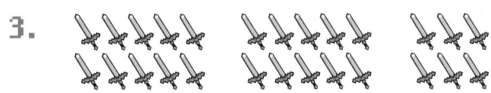

Answer: _____

5.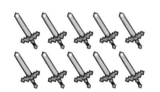

Answer: _____

MYSTERY MESSAGE
WITH ADDITION AND SUBTRACTION

Add or subtract. Then use the letters to fill in the blanks below and reveal the answer to Steve's joke.

1. $12 + 8 = 20$ H

2. $16 + 3 =$ _____ E

3. $11 - 8 =$ _____ A

4. $19 - 5 =$ _____ B

5. $14 + 3 =$ _____ Y

6. $16 + 2 =$ _____ N

7. $20 - 7 =$ _____ T

8. $18 - 3 =$ _____ D

9. $13 - 2 =$ _____ W

10. $17 - 9 =$ _____ O

11. $15 - 8 =$ _____ I

12. $12 + 4 =$ _____ G

Q: Why didn't the skeleton go to Alex's party?

COPY THE LETTERS FROM THE ANSWERS ABOVE TO FIND OUT.

H ___ H ___ ___ ___ ___
20 19 20 3 15 18 8

___ ___ ___ ___ ___ ___
14 8 15 17 13 8

___ ___ ___ ___ H ___
16 8 11 7 13 20

21

THE ENDERMAN NUMBER CHALLENGE

Match the Enderman with the description of the number.

1.

Tens	Ones
8	4

27 A.

2.

Tens	Ones
6	3

59 B.

3.

Tens	Ones
5	9

72 C.

4.

Tens	Ones
2	7

84 D.

5.

Tens	Ones
7	2

63 E.

SKIP COUNT CHALLENGE

Count by 10s to help tame the ocelot. Feed it enough fish on this numbered path and you'll have a new pet!

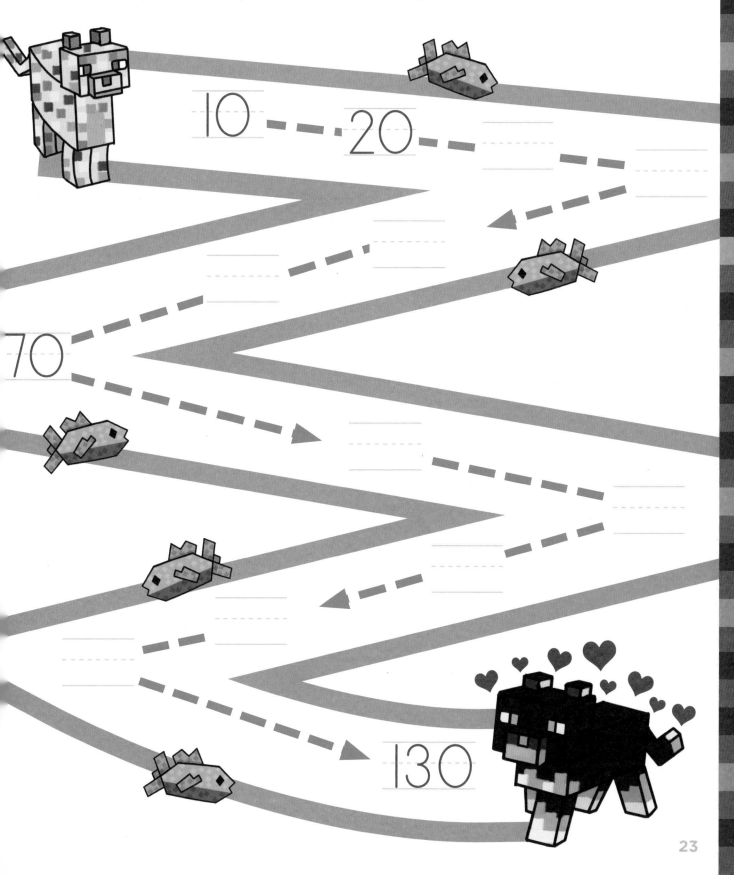

10 - - - 20 - - - _____
_____ _____
70 - - - _____
_____ _____ _____
_____ _____
_____ _____
_____ 130

THE TALLEST TOWER

Steve built 3 watchtowers in different sizes to help him find his way home. Compare the towers and write your answers below.

How many blocks tall is each tower?

A.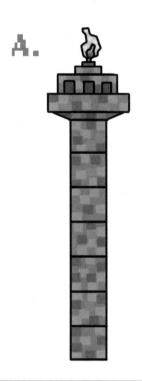

B.

C.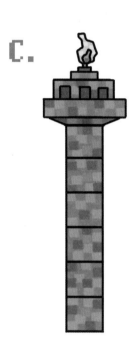

1. Which watchtower is the tallest?

2. Which watchtower is the shortest?

3. How much taller is watchtower A compared to watchtower B?

_____ **blocks.**

4. Draw your own watchtower, called watchtower D, in the space below. It must be taller than tower B, but shorter than tower C. Color it in using your favorite color!

D.

5. How many blocks tall is your watchtower? _____ **blocks.**

6. Fill in the rest of this table to keep track of all the different towers.

Tower	Number of Blocks Tall	Color
A	7	GRAY
B		
C		
D		

ADVENTURES IN GEOMETRY

Trace the dotted line to divide these shapes into 2 equal parts. Then color one half (½) of the shape.

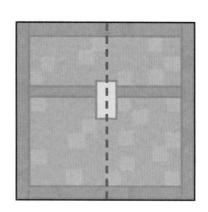

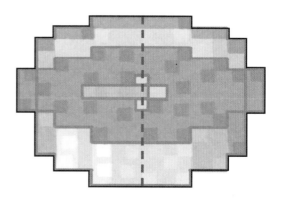

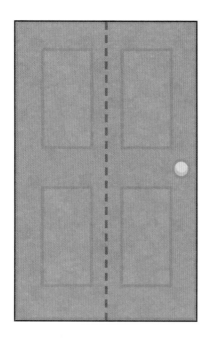

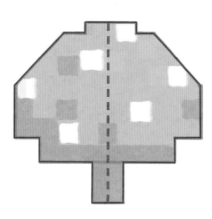

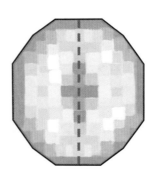

Trace the dotted line to divide these shapes into 4 equal parts. Then color in one quarter (¼) of each shape below.

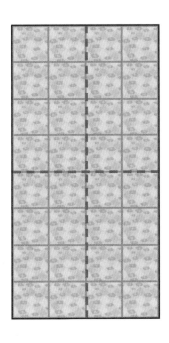

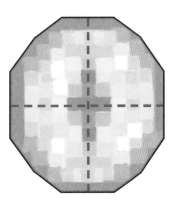

Color in one half of this wooden plank:

Color in one quarter of this wooden plank:

½

¼

WORD PROBLEMS

Read the problem carefully. Look at the picture and fill in your answer.

Example:

1. Steve eats 3 carrots. He attacks zombies, and they drop 2 more carrots and 2 potatoes for him to eat. How many food items does he eat all together?

 $3+2+2=7$

Answer: _7_

2. Alex gets 2 blocks of lava from a blacksmith's house, 5 more from the Nether, and 6 from an End Portal room. How many blocks of lava does she get in all?

Answer: _____

3. Steve sees 16 ghasts on his adventures. He destroys 4 with enchanted arrows and 3 more with fireballs. How many ghasts are left?

Answer: _____

4. In one day, Steve makes 10 pickaxes, 3 axes, and 9 shovels to attack mobs. How many weapons did he make in all?

Answer: _____

5. Alex gets 6 cookies from trading with a villager. She gets 7 more cookies later in the day and 4 more cookies in the morning. How many cookies does she have in all?

Answer: _____

6. You start your game with 20 hunger points. You lose 2 points running away from a creeper. You lose 4 more points attacking skeletons. How many hunger points are left?

Answer: _____

7. You start your game with 9 items in your inventory. You remove 4 tools and 2 food items. How many items are left in your inventory?

Answer: _____

8. Steve loves his pet cats. He has 4 in a fenced area outside, 7 in his house, and 5 in another fenced area. How many pet cats does he have?

Answer: _____

CREEPER'S GUIDE TO PLACE VALUE

Use the number on each creeper to fill in the place value chart.

Example:

1.
354

Hundreds	Tens	Ones
3	5	4

2.
760

Hundreds	Tens	Ones

3.
592

Hundreds	Tens	Ones

4.
184

Hundreds	Tens	Ones

5.
532

Hundreds	Tens	Ones

6.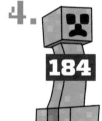
956

Hundreds	Tens	Ones

7.
453

Hundreds	Tens	Ones

SKIP COUNT CHALLENGE

Fill in the blank spaces as you count from 110 to 125 and help Alex find her way back to her house.

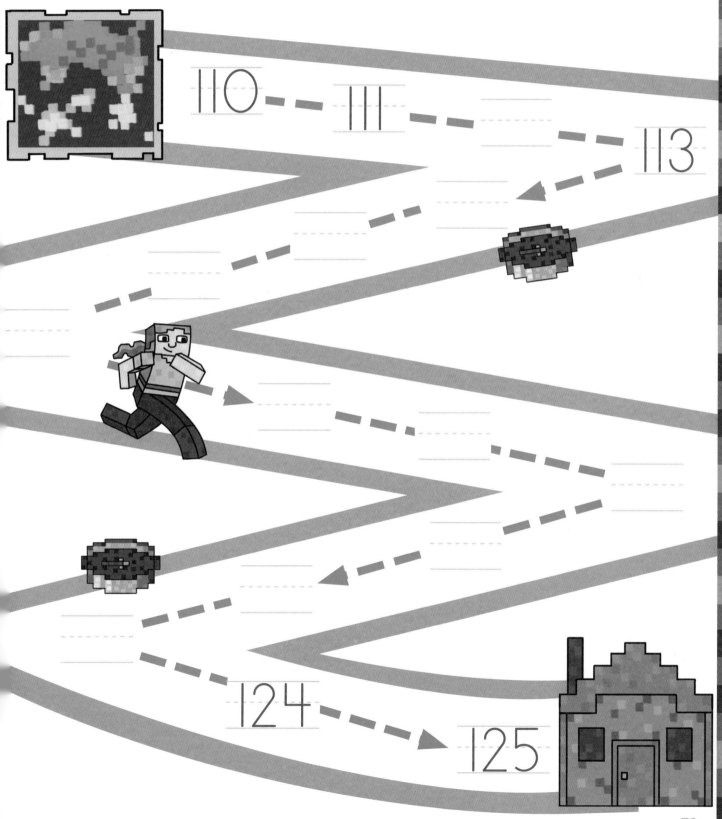

MOBS AND MONSTERS

Video game characters are sometimes called Mobs. Add an X to the boxes that describe each mob in the table below.

	Creeper	Zombie	Ghast	Enderman	Cave Spider	Snow Golem
0 Legs						
2 Legs						
More than 2 Legs						

Use the table to answer these questions.

1. How many Mobs have more than 2 legs? _____

2. How many Mobs have 2 legs or less? _____

3. Which 2 Mobs are the same color, but have a different number of legs and eyes? _____

COUNTING MONEY

Steve wants to feed his farm animals the following items. Find out how much money each item costs and write the amount in the space provided.

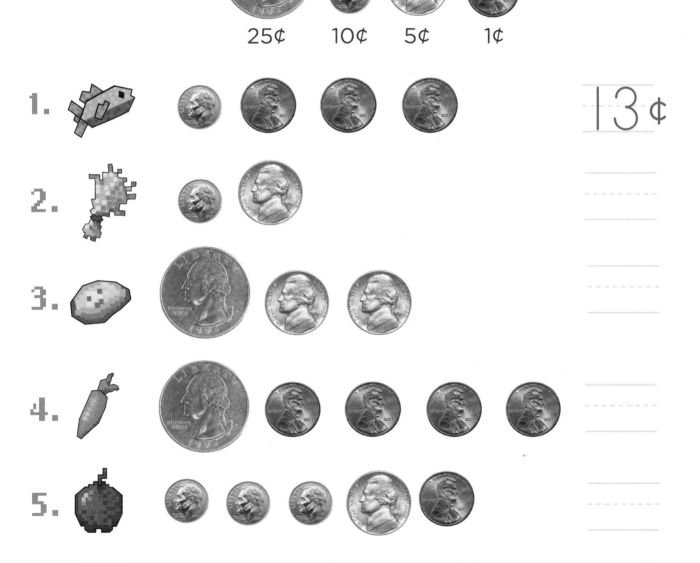

25¢   10¢   5¢   1¢

1. 13¢

2.

3.

4.

5.

HARDCORE MODE: *Try this hardcore math challenge!*

6. How much money does Steve need to buy all 7 of the food items listed above? Add them up to find out!

Answer:

ADVENTURES IN GEOMETRY: SPOT THE SHAPES

Look at the Minecrafter's house and answer the questions.
Use the shapes below to help you.

rectangle

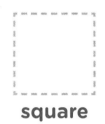

square

trapezoid

1. What shape is the roof of this house?

2. What shape is the double window?

3. What shape is the doorknob?

CREATIVE MODE

Use a pencil or pen to change the roof into a triangle!

Draw your own Minecrafter's house in the space below. Use as many shapes as you can. Add fun details and color!

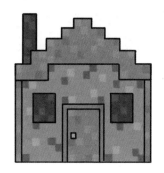

SANDSTONE ADDITION

Add the ones and then the tens to get the answer.

1.
```
  50
+ 26
```
D

2.
```
  72
+ 25
```
Q

3.
```
  43
+ 32
```
T

4.
```
  20
+ 64
```
E

5.
```
  82
+ 15
```
Z

6.
```
  90
+  8
```
S

7.
```
  83
+ 14
```
M

8.
```
  44
+ 30
```
E

9.
```
  25
+ 61
```
R

10.
```
  16
+ 43
```
B

11.
```
  24
+ 12
```
T

12.
```
  55
+ 54
```
K

HIDDEN MESSAGE:

Even numbers end in 0, 2, 4, 6, or 8. Circle the EVEN numbered answers above. Write the letter from those blocks in order from left to right below to spell out the name of a biome with lots of sandstone:

SUBTRACTION MYSTERY MESSAGE

Subtract the ones, then the tens. Use the letters to fill in the blanks below and answer Steve's riddle.

1. 45
   − 32
   _____
   S

2. 89
   − 45
   _____
   C

3. 93
   − 32
   _____
   O

4. 27
   − 12
   _____
   I

5. 32
   − 11
   _____
   U

6. 94
   − 23
   _____
   E

7. 48
   − 37
   _____
   F

8. 74
   − 32
   _____
   R

9. 68
   − 42
   _____
   M

10. 86
   − 33
   _____
   P

Q: What music does a creeper enjoy most?
Copy the letters from the answers above to find out!

___ ___ ___   ___ ___ ___ ___ ___
53 61 53   26 21 13 15 44

___ ___   ___ ___ ___ ___ ___ ___
61 11   44 61 21 42 13 71

MOB MONSTER SHOWDOWN

Who has more attack power? Compare the number of times each Mob has attacked a player and write in the correct symbol.

> means greater than   **< means less than**

Example **1.** 385 < 392

2. 856 ___ 826

3. 445 ___ 454

4. 523 ___ 527

5. 672 ___ 607

6. 908 ___ 998

7. 746 ___ 772

Count up their wins and circle the one with the most wins below.

Skeleton   **Enderman**

SKIP COUNT CHALLENGE

Count by 3s to collect all of the ink from the squids.

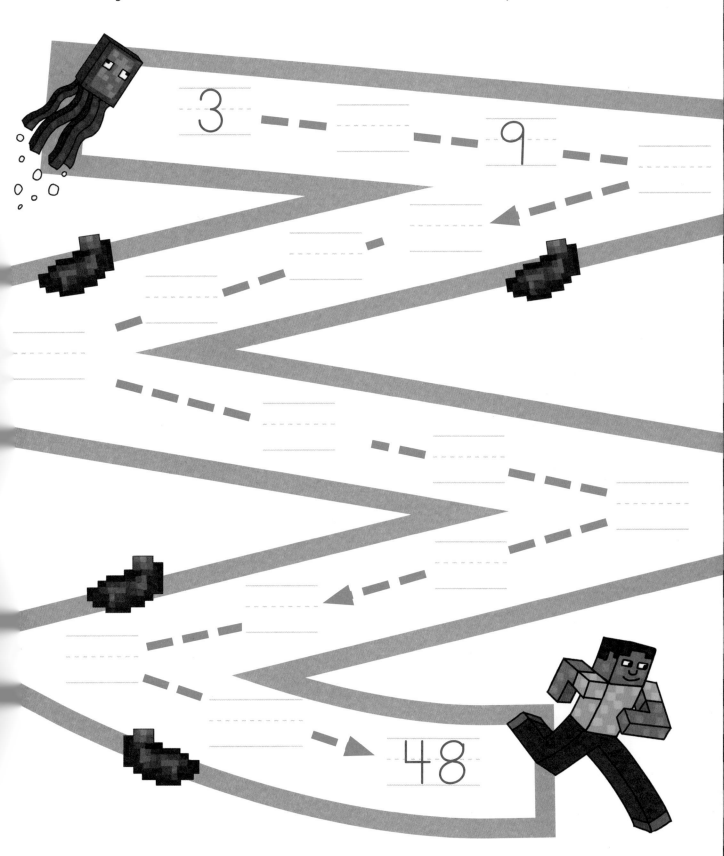

3 ... 9 ... 48

TELLING TIME

Look at the clocks below and write the time in the space provided:

Example:

1.

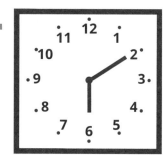

Answer: 2:45

2.

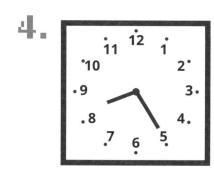

Answer:

3.

Answer:

4.

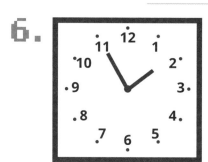

Answer:

5.

Answer:

6.

Answer:

7.

Answer: _____

8.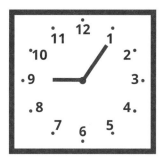

Answer: _____

9.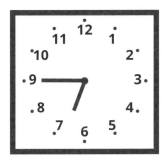

Answer: _____

10.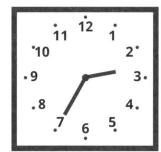

Answer: _____

11.

Answer: _____

12.

Answer: _____

13.

Answer: _____

14.

Answer: _____

4 SIDES ARE BETTER THAN 1

A Minecrafter's world is full of **quadrilaterals**. Find them and circle them below.

Hint: Quadrilaterals are closed shapes with 4 sides. Squares and rectangles are two kinds of quadrilaterals.

Can you find 3 purple quadrilaterals on this fish?

Can you find...
...9 quadrilaterals in this treasure chest?

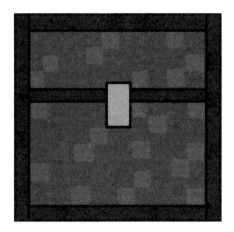

...7 quadrilaterals in this Minecrafter's house?

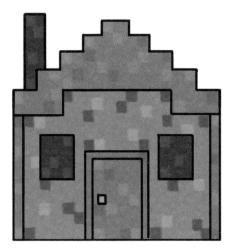

Trace the quadrilaterals below:

ADDITION & SUBTRACTION MYSTERY NUMBER

There is a number hidden behind these redstone blocks.
Subtract or count on to find the mystery number.

1.
```
   15
 +  ■
 ─────
   18
```
■ = 3

2.
```
   22
 +  ■
 ─────
   29
```
■ =

3.
```
   43
 +  ■
 ─────
   53
```
■ =

4.
```
   17
 +  ■
 ─────
   25
```
■ =

5.
```
   76
 +  ■
 ─────
   82
```
■ =

6.
```
   50
 +  ■
 ─────
   64
```
■ =

7.
```
   49
 +  ■
 ─────
   56
```
■ =

8.
```
   27
 +  ■
 ─────
   30
```
■ =

9.
```
   63
 +  ■
 ─────
   70
```
■ =

MYSTERY MESSAGE
WITH ADDITION USING REGROUPING

Add. Use the letters to fill in the blanks below and answer the riddle.

1. 45
   + 9
   ____
    O

2. 89
   + 7
   ____
    T

3. 33
   + 8
   ____
    N

4. 27
   + 13
   ____
    E

5. 38
   + 6
   ____
    I

6. 25
   + 6
   ____
    F

7. 46
   + 27
   ____
    R

8. 74
   + 19
   ____
    H

9. 28
   + 42
   ____
    S

10. 56
   + 16
   ____
    A

Q: How many pieces of armor can you fit in an empty treasure chest?

____ ____ ____ .   ____ ____ ____ ____ ____
 54   41   40   72   31   96   40   73

____ ____ ____ ____   ____ ____ ____ ,
 96   93   72   96   44   96   70

____ ____ ____ ____   M   P   ____   Y .
 41   54   96   40   96

45

PIGMAN'S GUIDE TO PLACE VALUE

Identify the number that belongs in the place-value chart and write it there.

Example:

1.  **5 4**

Tens
3

2.  **973**

Hundreds

3.  **462**

Ones

4.  **875**

Hundreds

5. **546**

Tens

6.  **231**

Ones

7.  **952**

Hundreds

SKIP COUNT CHALLENGE

Enter The End through The End portal and count by
4s until you reach the Enderdragon for an epic battle.

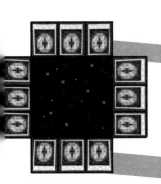

4 — 8 — 16

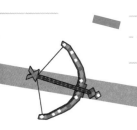

60

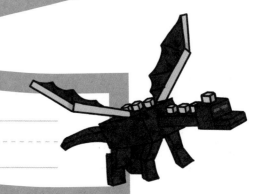

ANIMAL TALLY

Use the table to compare the animals that Alex and Steve have on their farms.

	🐔	🐑	🐷	🐄
STEVE	III	II	HHT II	HHT HHT
ALEX	IIII	HHT I	HHT	HHT

1. How many sheep does Alex keep on her farm?

2. Who has more pigs, Steve or Alex?

3. Steve and Alex both have cows. How many *more* cows does Steve have?

4. If Steve and Alex put their chickens together on one farm, how many chickens would they have?

WEAPON TALLY

Use the table to compare the weapons that Steve and Alex have crafted.

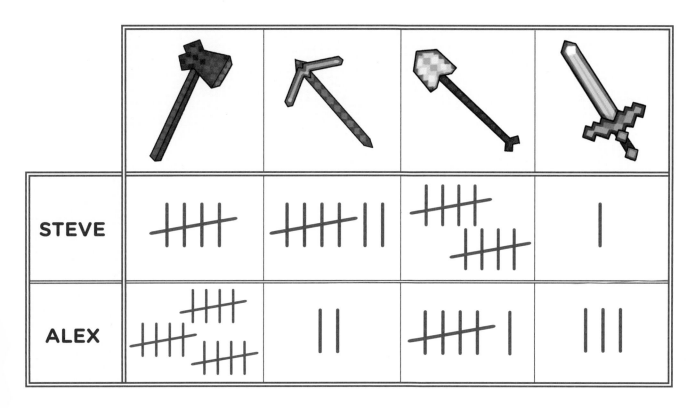

	Axe	Pickaxe	Shovel	Sword
STEVE	卌	卌 卌 II	卌 卌 卌	I
ALEX	卌 卌 卌 卌	II	卌 卌 I	III

1. How many shovels did Steve craft?

2. Steve and Alex both have diamond swords. How many *more* diamond swords does Alex have?

3. Steve and Alex both have axes. How many *more* axes does Alex have?

4. Who has the most pickaxes?

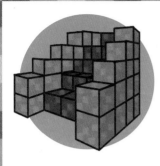

ADVENTURES IN GEOMETRY: SPOT THE SHAPES

Can you spot: 14 **triangles** in this pile of gems?

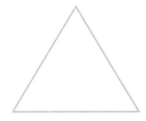

Can you spot: 6 **trapezoids** in this diamond armor?

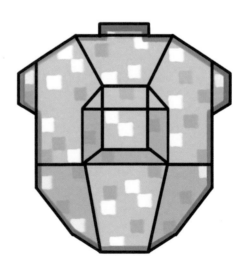

Use the words in the inventory bar to answer these questions.

| octagon | quadrilateral | oval | sphere | cube |

1. Which shape will this treasure chest be when it is closed?

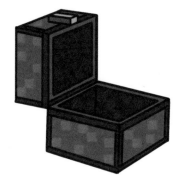

_____

2. Which shape always has 4 sides?

_____

3. Which shape is the face of this Minecraft clock?

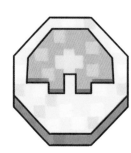

_____

4. Which shape is a 3-D circle, like a round ball?

_____

5. What shape best describes this egg?

_____

WORD PROBLEMS

Write a number sentence to help you solve these word problems.

Example:

1. You break 13 dirt blocks with your diamond shovel. You also break 5 sand blocks and 3 gravel blocks. How many blocks do you break in all?

$$13 + 5 + 3 = 21$$

Answer: 21 blocks

2. You get 17 mushrooms to make a stew. A cow eats 3 of them. You get 5 more mushrooms. How many mushrooms do you have now?

Answer: _____

3. You make 6 snow golems to protect your house. A zombie destroys 2 of them. You make 7 more. How many snow golems do you have now?

Answer: _____

4. You are being followed by 9 zombie villagers. You start running, but 9 more zombie villagers join them. You destroy 4 zombie villagers. How many zombie villagers are left?

Answer:

5. You destroy some Endermen and get 30 Eyes of Ender. You use 12 to activate the End Portal. How many Eyes of Ender do you have left?

Answer:

6. In the Nether, a ghast shoots 13 fireballs at you. Another ghast shoots 15 more fireballs at you. Before you can escape, it shoots 2 more fireballs at you. How many fireballs were shot at you?

Answer:

7. Your house is made of 52 cobblestone blocks. An Enderman steals 7 blocks from your house. The next night, he steals 5 more blocks. How many blocks are left?

Answer:

IRON GOLEM'S GUIDE TO PLACE VALUE

Match the number on each Iron Golem to the place value descriptions on the right.

Example:

1.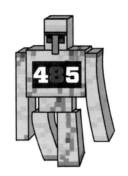

Tens
8

2.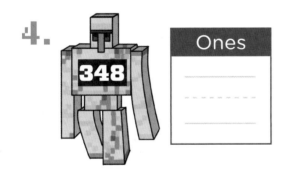

Ones

3.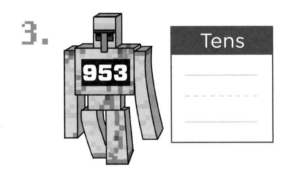

Tens

4.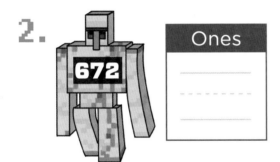

Ones

5.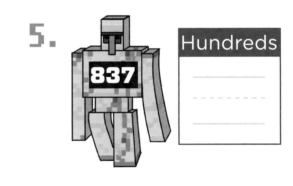

Hundreds

6.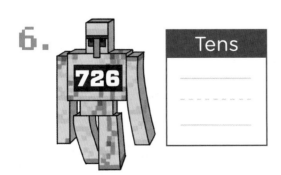

Tens

7.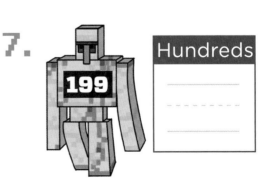

Hundreds

SKIP COUNT CHALLENGE

Count by 100s to fill in the path and help tame this wolf with raw meat.

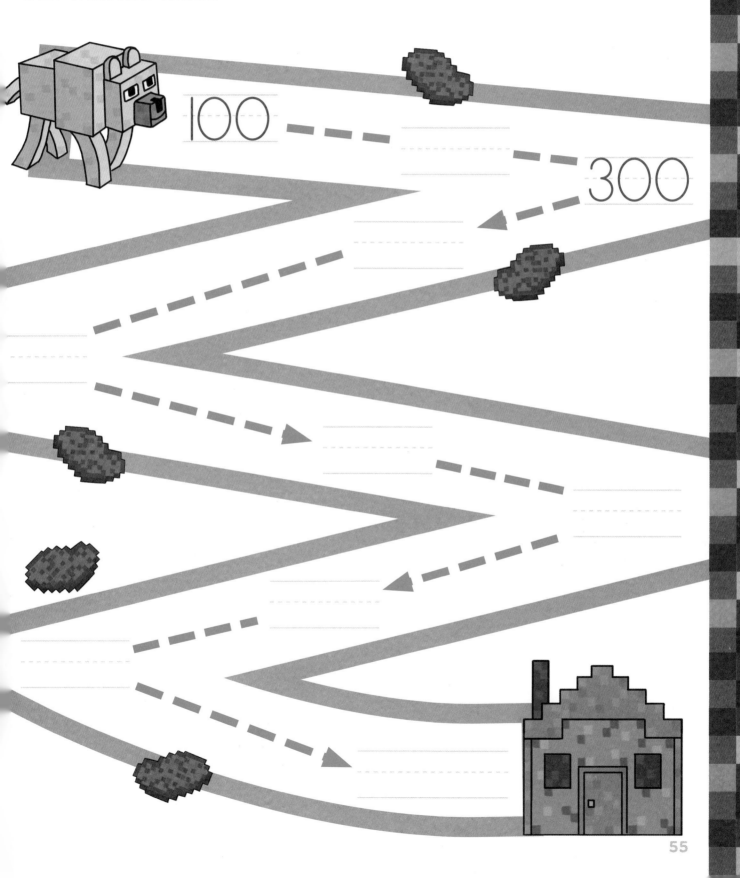

100

300

TELLING TIME

Look at the clocks below and write the time in the space provided

1.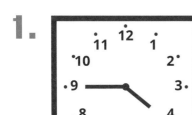

Answer: 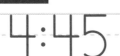 4:45

2.

Answer:

3.

Answer:

4.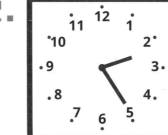

Answer:

5.

Answer:

6.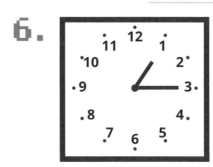

Answer:

COUNTING MONEY

How much money is hidden in each treasure chest? Add up the coins to find out.

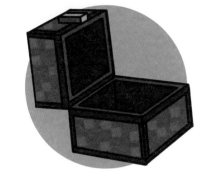

25¢   10¢   5¢   1¢

1.    4|1 ¢

2.

3.

4.

5.

HARDCORE MODE: Try this hardcore math challenge!

Steve looks in a treasure chest and finds 4 coins that add up to 40¢. There is only 1 kind of coin in the treasure chest. What coin is it?

57

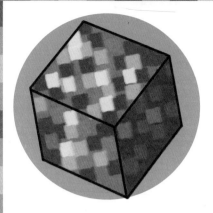

GEOMETRY

This wooden plank is divided into 4 equal parts called fourths. Color the wooden planks below according to the description.

1. Color: one fourth

$\frac{1}{4}$

2. Color: three fourths

$\frac{3}{4}$

3. Color: two fourths

$\frac{2}{4}$

4. Color: four fourths

$\frac{4}{4}$

5. Which set of planks above is the same as one half?

Match the shaded set of blocks to the correct fraction on the right.

6. $\dfrac{5}{8}$

7. $\dfrac{3}{8}$

8. $\dfrac{2}{8}$

9. $\dfrac{4}{8}$

10. $\dfrac{1}{8}$

ANSWERS

Page 4: Addition By Grouping
2. 16
3. 31
4. 21
5. 17

Page 5: Mystery Message with Addition and Subtraction
2. 3
3. 11
4. 2
5. 13
6. 6
7. 15
8. 7
9. 14
A: Because they have bad STABLE MANNERS

Page 6: Zombie's Guide to Place Value
2. 4 tens 5 ones
3. 2 tens 5 ones
4. 3 tens 1 one
5. 2 tens 8 ones
6. 6 tens 7 ones
7. 5 tens 4 ones

Page 7: Skip Count Challenge
8, 10, 12, 14, 16, 18, 20, 22, 24

Page 8: Telling Time
2. 4:30
3. 11:00
4. 9:30
5. 7:30
6. 5:00

Page 9: Counting Money
2. 23 cents
3. 36 cents
4. 60 cents
5. 37 cents

6. 41 cents
7. 9 cents
Hardcore Mode:
8. 5 nickels

Page 10: Adventures in Geometry
2.

3. 9

Page 11:
4.

5.

6. Hardcore Mode: $\frac{1}{2}$

Page 12: Word Problems
1. 1
2. 5
3. 4

Page 13:
4. 8
5. 11
6. 6
7. 9
8. 3

Page 14: Ghast's Guide to Place Value
2. 4 tens, 3 ones
3. 3 tens, 5 ones
4. 2 tens, 9 ones
5. 4 tens, 7 ones
6. 8 tens, 9 ones
7. 6 tens, 3 ones

Page 15: Skip Count Challenge
20, 25, 30, 35, 40, 45, 50, 55, 60

Page 16: All in a Day's Work

2. G
3. F
4. C
5. A
6. B
7. D

Page 17: Time for Matching

Page 18: Learning About Shapes:

1. C
2. A
3. D
4. B

Page 19: Find the Shapes

5. Rectangle
6. Square
7. Circle
8.

Page 20: Addition by Grouping

2. 32
3. 26
4. 28
5. 19

Page 21: Mystery Message with Addition and Subtraction

2. 19
3. 3
4. 14
5. 17
6. 18
7. 13
8. 15
9. 11
10. 8
11. 7
12. 16

A: HE HAD NO BODY TO GO WITH

Page 22: The Enderman Number Challenge

1. D
2. E
3. B
4. A
5. C

Page 23: Skip Count Challenge

30, 40, 50, 60; 80, 90, 100, 110, 120

Page 24: The Tallest Tower

a. 7 Blocks
b. 4 Blocks
c. 6 Blocks

1. A
2. B
3. 3 Blocks

Page 25: The Tallest Tower, cont'd

Tower	Number of Blocks Tall	Color
A	7	GRAY
B	4	GRAY
C	6	GRAY
D		

Page 27: Adventures in Geometry

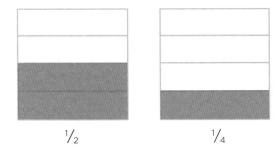

½   ¼

Page 28-29: Word Problems

2. 13 blocks of lava
3. 9 ghasts
4. 22 weapons
5. 17 cookies
6. 14 hunger points
7. 3 items
8. 16 pet cats

Page 30: Creeper's Guide to Place Value

2. Hundreds:7 Tens:6 Ones:0
3. Hundreds:5 Tens:9 Ones:2
4. Hundreds:1 Tens:8 Ones:4
5. Hundreds:5 Tens:3 Ones:2
6. Hundreds:9 Tens:5 Ones:6
7. Hundreds:4 Tens:5 Ones:3

Page 31: Skip Count Challenge

112; 114, 115, 116, 117, 118, 119, 120, 121, 122, 123

Page 32: Mobs and Monsters

	Creeper	Zombie	Ghast	Enderman	Cave Spider	Snow Golem
0 Legs	X					X
2 Legs		X		X		
More than 2 Legs			X		X	

1. 2 legs
2. 4 legs
3. Enderman and Cave Spider

Page 33: Counting Money

1. 13 cents
2. 15 cents
3. 35 cents
4. 29 cents
5. 36 cents

Hardcore Mode: 6. 128 cents, or $1.28

Page 34: Adventures in Geometry: Spot the Shapes

1. Trapezoid
2. Rectangle
3. Square

Page 36: Sandstone Addition

1. 76
2. 97
3. 75
4. 84
5. 97
6. 98
7. 97
8. 74
9. 86
10. 59
11. 36
12. 109

Hidden Message: DESERT

Page 37: Subtraction Mystery Message

1. 13
2. 44
3. 61
4. 15

5. 21

6. 71

7. 11

8. 42

9. 26

10. 53

A: POP MUSIC, OF COURSE

Page 38: Mob Monster Showdown

1. <

2. >

3. <

4. <

5. >

6. <

7. <

Enderman

Page 39: Skip Count Challenge

6, 12, 15, 18, 21, 24, 27, 30, 33, 36, 39, 42, 45

Page 40: Telling Time

2. 4:15

3. 6:10

4. 8:25

5. 3:50

6. 1:55

7. 12:40

8. 9:05

9. 6:45

10. 2:35

11. 1:10

12. 10:25

13. 5:55

14. 6:40

Page 42: 4 Sides are Better Than 1

1.

2.

3.

Page 44: Addition & Subtraction Mystery Number

1. 3

2. 7

3. 10

4. 8

5. 6

6. 14

7. 7

8. 3

9. 7

Page 45: Mystery Message with Addition Using Regrouping

1. 54

2. 96

3. 41

4. 40

5. 44

6. 31

7. 73

8. 93

9. 70

10. 72

A: ONE. AFTER THAT IT'S NOT EMPTY.

Page 46: Pigman's Guide to Place Value

1. 3

2. 9

3. 2

4. 8

5. 4

6. 1

7. 9

Page 47: Skip Count Challenge

12; 20, 24, 28, 32, 36, 40, 44, 48, 52, 56, 64, 68

Page 48: Animal Tally

    1. 6

    2. Steve

    3. 5

    4. 7

Page 49: Weapons Tally

    1. 10

    2. 2

    3. 10

    4. Steve

Page 50: Spot the Shapes

1.

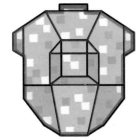

2.

Page 51: Adventures in Geometry: Spot the Shape

    1. Cube

    2. Quadrilateral

    3. Octagon

    4. Sphere

    5. Oval

Page 52: Word Problems

    2. 19 mushrooms

    3. 11 snow golems

    4. 14 zombie villagers

    5. 18 eyes of Ender

    6. 30 fireballs

    7. 40 cobblestone blocks

Page 54: Iron Golem's Guide to Place Value

    2. 2

    3. 5

    4. 8

    5. 8

    6. 2

    7. 1

Page 55: Skip Count

200; 400, 500, 600, 700, 800, 900, 1000

Page 56: Telling Time

    2. 2:25

    3. 7:50

    4. 8:05

    5. 9:35

    6. 1:15

Page 57: Counting Money

    2. 60 cents

    3. 39 cents

    4. 42 cents

    5. 83 cents

Hardcore Mode:

    6. Dime

Page 58-59: Geometry

    5. Two fourths

    6. $\frac{1}{8}$

    7. $\frac{2}{8}$

    8. $\frac{3}{8}$

    9. $\frac{4}{8}$

    10. $\frac{5}{8}$